Little Skill Seekers

ALPHABET

SCHOLASTIC

New York • Toronto • London • Auckland • Sydney • New Delhi
Mexico City • Hong Kong • Buenos Aires

Cover Design: Tannaz Fassihi
Cover Illustration: Michael Robertson
Interior Design: Mina Chen
Interior Illustration: Doug Jones

ISBN: 978-1-338-25552-2

2 3 4 5 6 7 8 9 10   40   24 23 22 21 20 19

Dear Parent,

Welcome to *Little Skill Seekers: Alphabet*! Recognizing letters and letter-sound relationships are important early literacy skills—this workbook will help your child develop these skills.

Help your little skill seeker build a strong foundation for learning by choosing more books in the Little Skill Seekers series. The exciting and colorful workbooks in the series are designed to set your child on the path to success. Each book targets essential skills important to your child's development.

Here are some key features of *Little Skill Seekers: Alphabet* and the other workbooks in this series:

- Filled with colorful illustrations that make learning fun and playful

- Provides plenty of opportunity to practice essential skills

- Builds independence as children work through the pages on their own, at their own pace

- Comes in a perfect size that fits easily in a backpack for practice on the go

Now let's get started on this journey to help your child become a successful, lifelong learner!

—The Editors

A is for Apple.

Trace and write A and a.

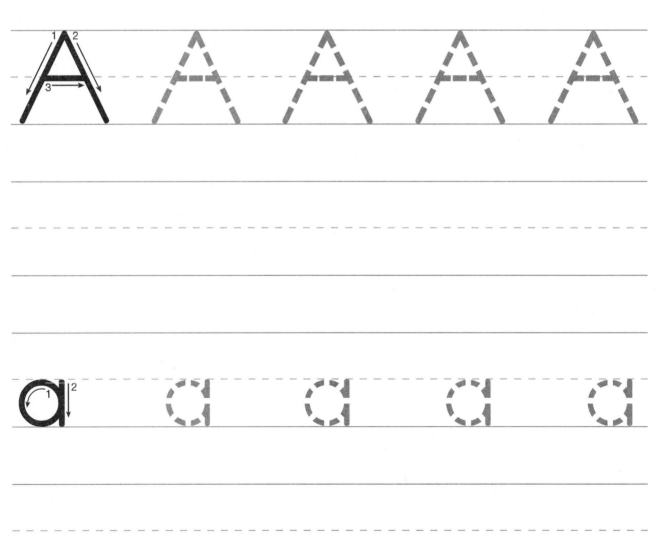

Bb

B is for Boy.

Trace and write B and b.

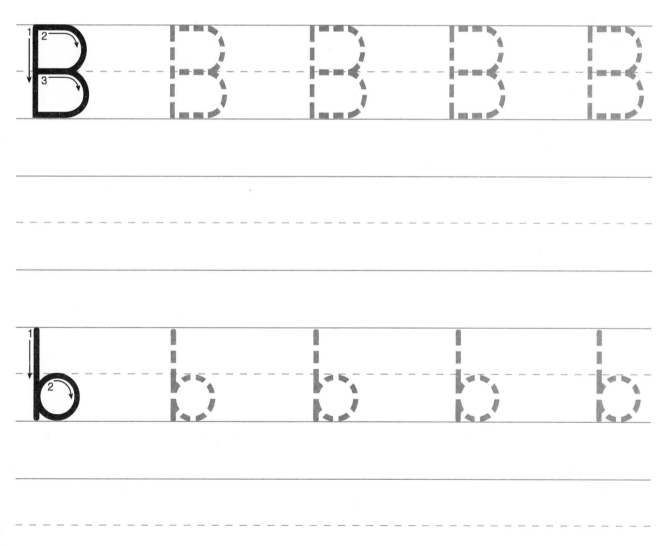

C is for Carrot.

Trace and write C and c.

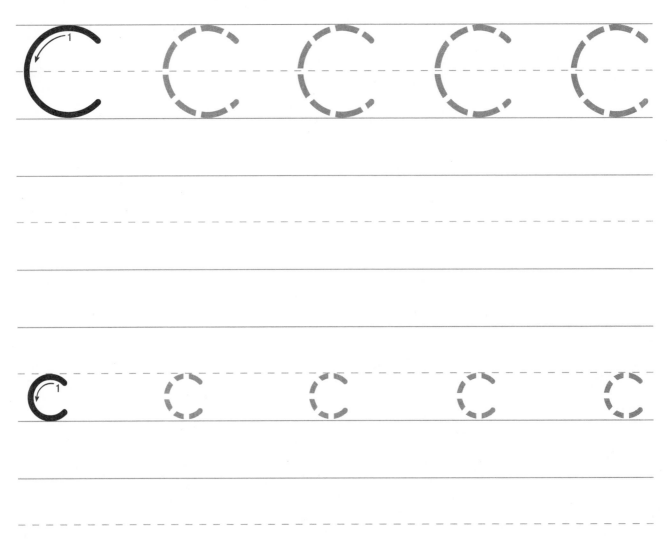

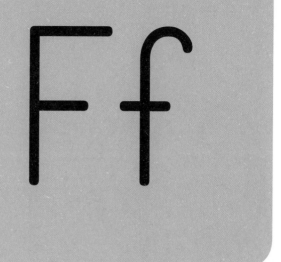

F is for Frog.

Trace and write F and f.

G is for Girl.

Trace and write G and g.

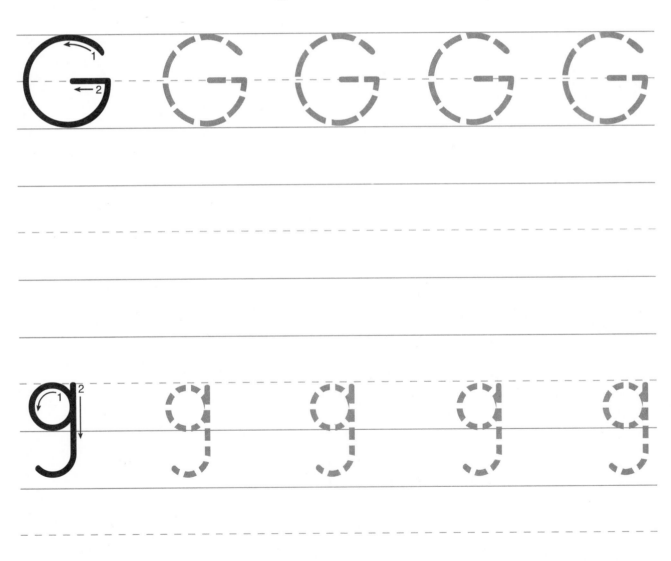

Match uppercase letters to lowercase letters.

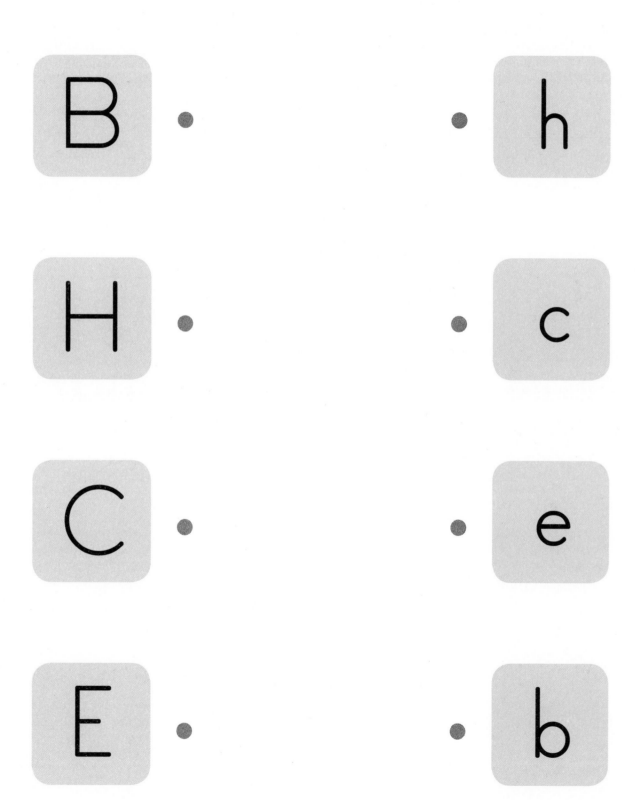

Circle the first letter in the animal's name.
Write the letter to finish the word.

e   a   o   _____ lephant

t   p   c   _____ at

14

Circle the first letter in the animal's name.
Write the letter to finish the word.

b   c   r   ____ ee

j   p   h   ____ ippo

15

Circle the first letter in the animal's name.
Write the letter to finish the word.

l   a   g   _____ lligator

w   f   r   _____ ox

Circle the first letter in the animal's name.
Write the letter to finish the word.

g t k   _____ oat

l d n   _____ uck

17

I i

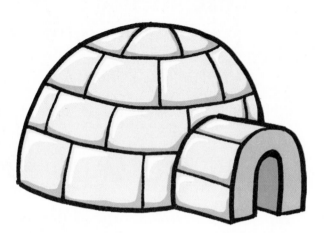

Trace and write I and i.

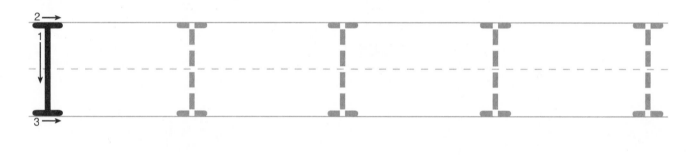

L l

L is for Leaf.

Trace and write L and l.

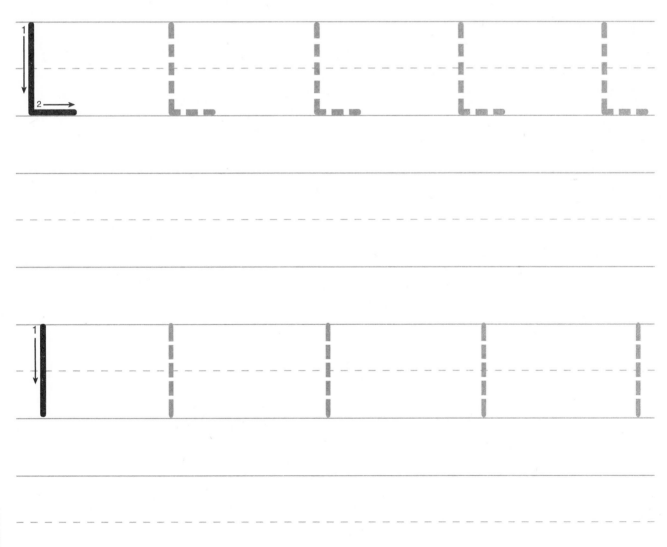

M is for Man.

Trace and write M and m.

N is for Nest.

Trace and write N and n.

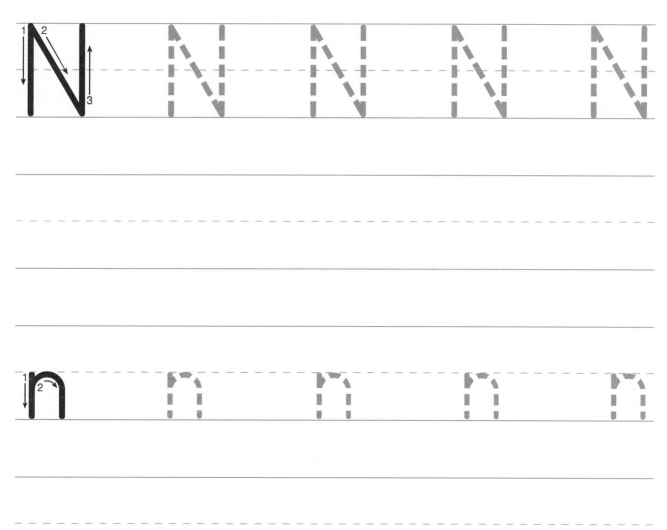

O is for Ostrich.

Trace and write O and o.

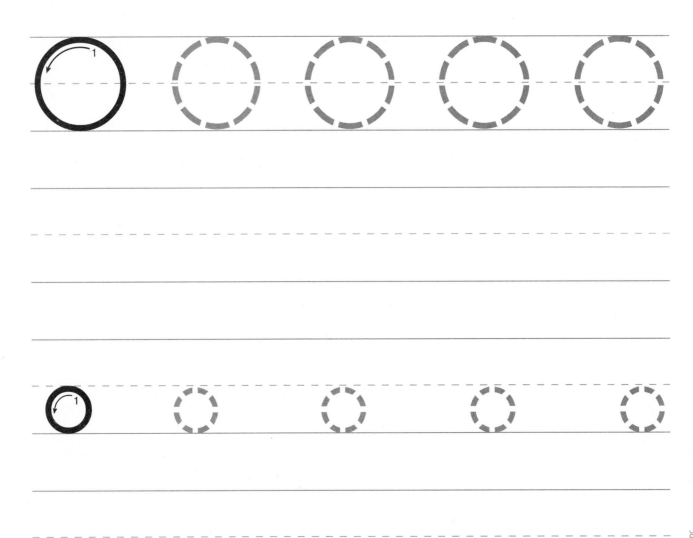

Pp

Trace and write P and p.

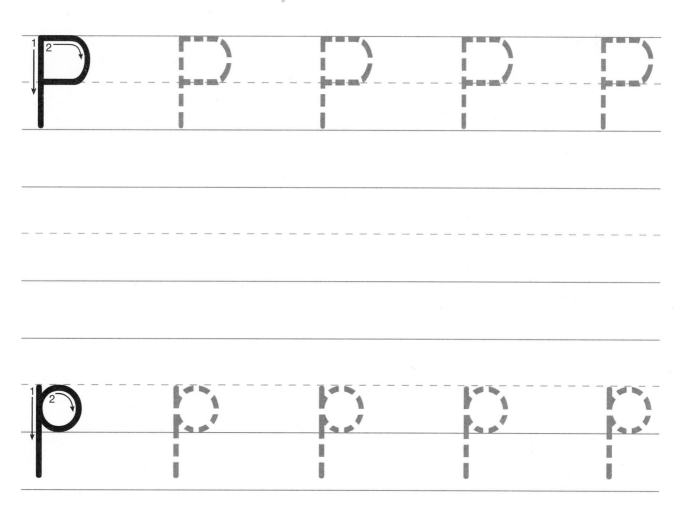

Match uppercase letters to lowercase letters.

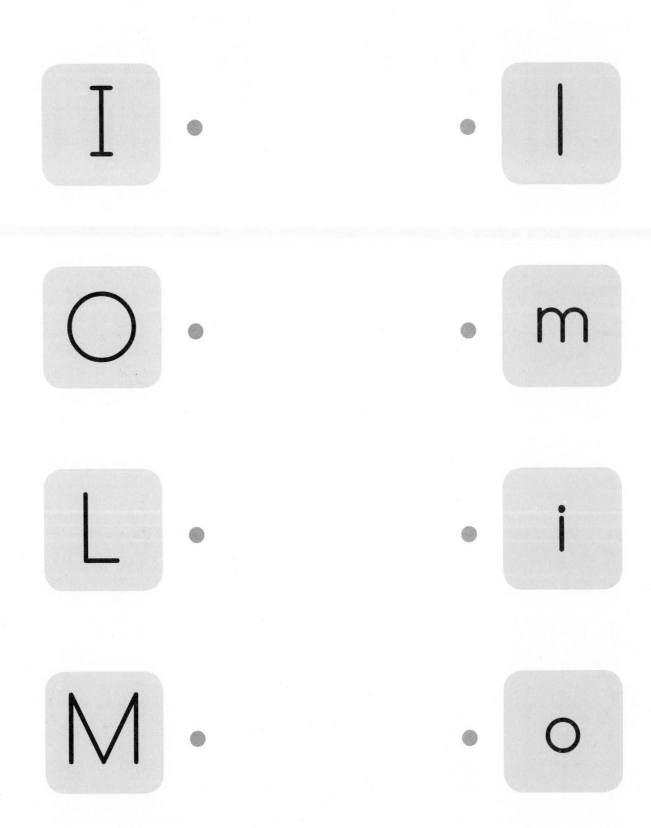

Match uppercase letters to lowercase letters.

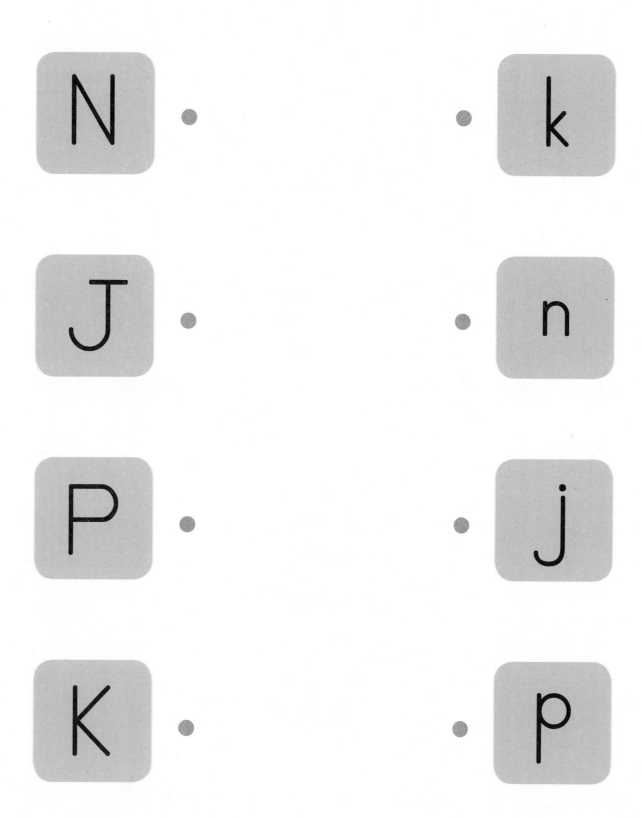

Circle the first letter in the animal's name.
Write the letter to finish the word.

i   e   a   _____ guana

p   d   c   _____ anda

28

**Circle the first letter in the animal's name.
Write the letter to finish the word.**

a   a e o   _____ wl

l   l p s   _____ adybug

Circle the first letter in the animal's name.
Write the letter to finish the word.

n　l　r

_____ewt

j　h　k

_____angaroo

Circle the first letter in the animal's name.
Write the letter to finish the word.

k   m   n   _____ onkey

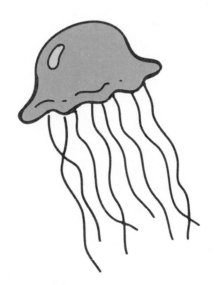

p   d   j   _____ ellyfish

Q is for Queen.

Trace and write Q and q.

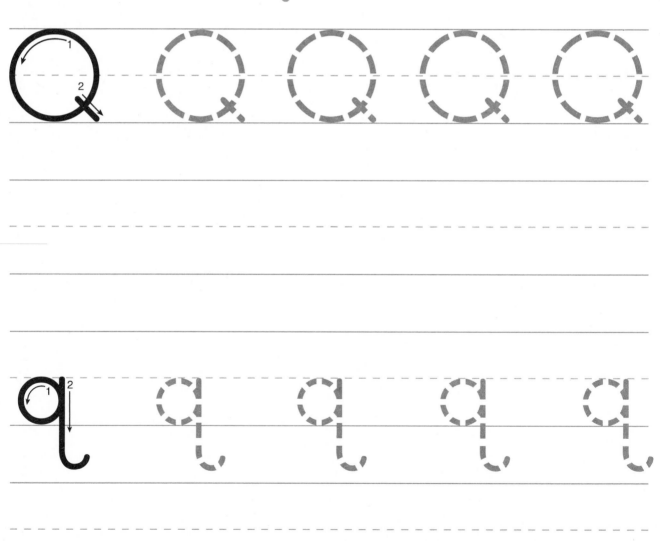

32

© Scholastic Inc.

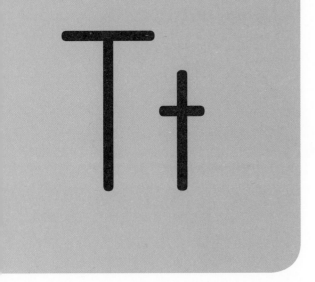

T is for Tree.

Trace and write T and t.

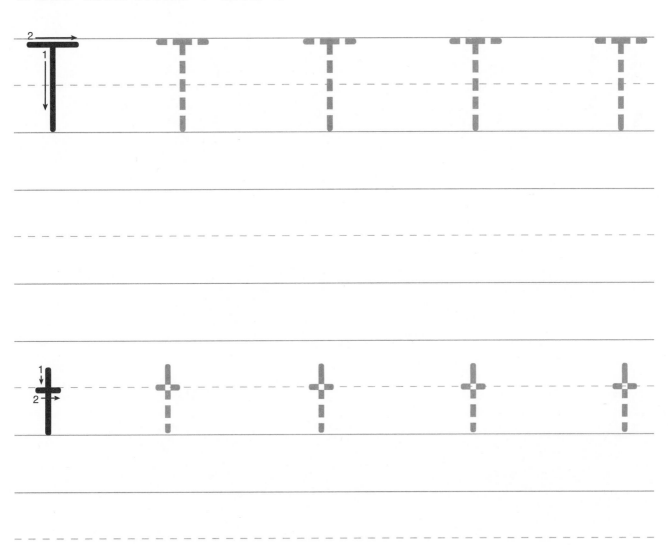

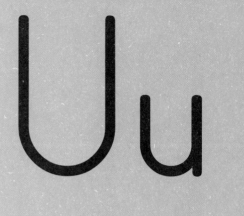

U is for Umbrella.

Trace and write U and u.

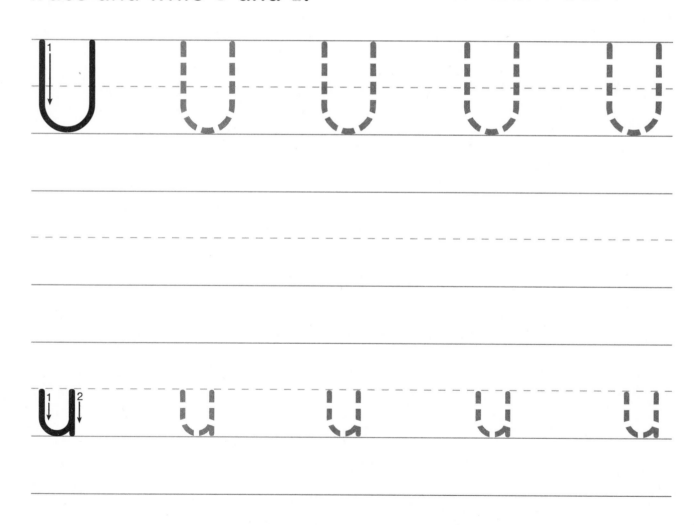

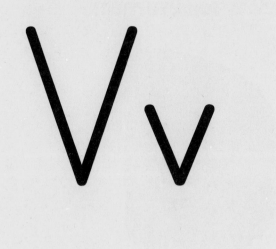

V is for Violin.

Trace and write V and v.

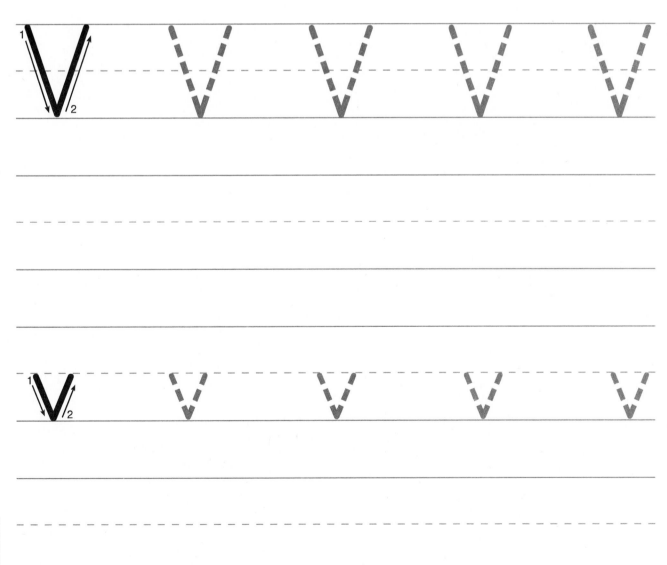

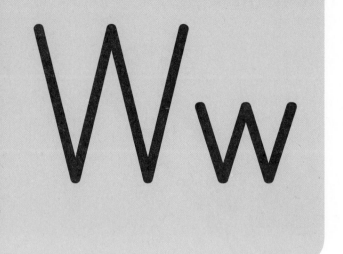

W is for Woman.

Trace and write W and w.

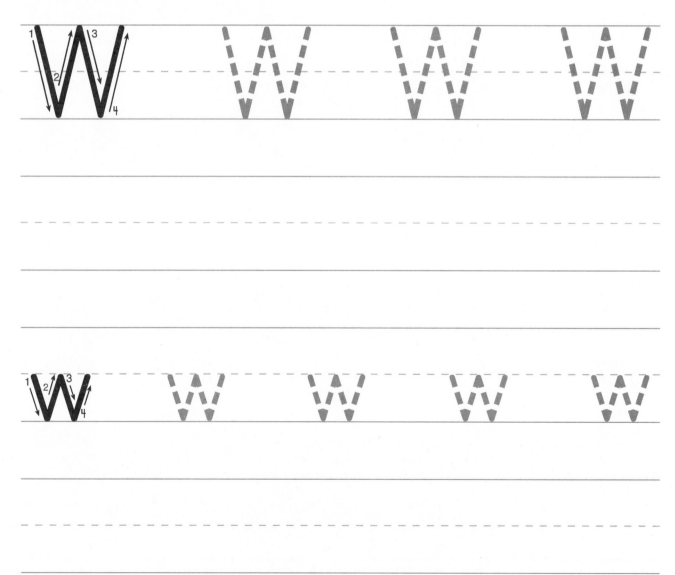

Match uppercase letters to lowercase letters.

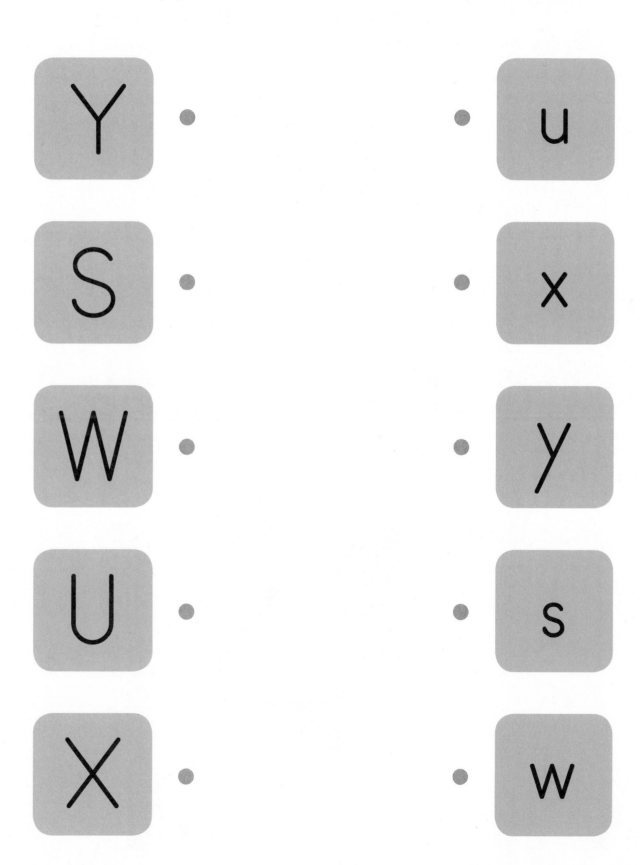

Circle the first letter in the animal's name.
Write the letter to finish the word.

c   r   t   _____ abbit

q   d   e   _____ uail

Circle the first letter in the animal's name.
Write the letter to finish the word.

v c n

_____ulture

y w g

_____ak

Circle the first letter in the animal's name.
Write the letter to finish the word.

k **z** **c** _____ebra

l **r** **x** _____-ray fish

Circle the first letter in the animal's name.
Write the letter to finish the word.

w   h   s

____hale

h   t   s

____heep

47

Circle the first letter in the animal's name.
Write the letter to finish the word.

e   u   y   ____nicorn

t   z   o   ____urtle